W9-AUJ-543

Contents

3023   1/98 durer 4/0

Temper, Temper

I have observed that there are two kinds of cowboys in this world. The first kind is young and foolish. He expects livestock to do what he wants them to do. He expects his work to go smoothly and according to plan. When it doesn't, he loses his temper and often curses.

The second kind of cowboy is old and foolish. He expects exactly the same things, even though he's old enough to know better, and he loses his temper and curses too.

The major difference between the two is that when the young cowboy loses his temper, he often takes actions which hurt himself more than they hurt the animals he's mad at. The older cowboy, somewhat wiser for his years of experience, will think twice before he lashes out in rage. If any blood is to be shed, he will see to it that it's not his.

One of the dumbest stunts I ever heard of a young cowboy pulling involved a fellow named Erickson, who happens to be the writer of this article. It occurred on a very hot summer day in 1974.

I was cowboying in Beaver County, Oklahoma, back then. A cow and calf belonging to one of the neighbors had strayed into one of our pastures and had enjoyed free room and board for several weeks. I decided it was time for them to leave.

I saddled old Reno and off we went to throw the rascals out. When they saw me coming, the cow went north and the calf went south. I ran the cow all the way to the hole in the fence (she knew exactly where it was), and then I went back for the calf. I had already decided that he needed roping.

He weighed about two hundred pounds. He could run like a deer and dodge like a jackrabbit, and he made a complete monkey out of me and my catch rope. When I finally got him caught, I was in a towering rage.

I flanked him down and started tying him with my pigging string. He kicked out of it. I tried again, and he kicked out again. Then he kicked *me*. Sweat was stinging my eyes, so I couldn't see too well. I cocked my fist and aimed a right hook at his neck. He squirmed, and the blow landed squarely between his horns—the very hardest part of his anatomy.

I wish I could report that he shuddered, stiffened, and died on the spot, but that would be an exaggeration. Instead, I howled and drew back a withered limb. For the next six weeks, I had to explain how I got the plaster cast on my right hand.

No matter how well I told the story or how hard I tried to improve it, I couldn't quite conceal the truth of it—that it was a pretty stupid thing for a grown man to do.

But my pal High Loper understood, even if nobody else did, because, like me, Loper was young and foolish and had recently pulled a stunt of his own.

He was trying to break a horse named Macho, a big, stout, gorgeous gelding that had all the physical qualities you want in a ranch horse. But he had one small flaw: he hated saddles, blankets, bridles, corrals, and cowboys.

Cowboys who end up with a horse like Macho dream of selling him to an enemy. If they ever talk to a buyer about him, they will say, "Shoot, all this horse needs is a lot of miles." Which means, "Ride him fifty miles a day in a sandy river bottom, seven days a week, and maybe he won't kill you."

One day in the saddle lot Macho went on a snort, and when the dust cleared, he had the saddle under his belly and he had built a couple of new gates in the corral fence. Outraged, High Loper stomped over to the horse and taught him a lesson. He kicked him in the butt and broke his big toe.

Not long after this, Macho was sold and went to "a big ranch up north," as Loper puts it. If that doesn't mean "to the packers," then the dirty son of a gun got better than he deserved.

High Loper and I were young and foolish back then. Had we been wiser, we might have followed the example of men who had outgrown their urge to kick, slug, and bite animals that shouldn't be kicked, slugged, or bitten.

Consider the example set by a cowboy I knew up in the Oklahoma Panhandle. One day many years ago he was trying to drive a bull to the headquarters

3

corrals. The bull went on the prod and tried to hook the horse. This man was too old for silly displays of temper, which to his mind included sticking a rope on something as big and evil as a Hereford bull.

He didn't lose his temper. He rode to the barn and came back armed with a pitchfork. The next time the old bull took a razzoo at the horse, he got acquainted with a five-tine fork, and when he turned to run, he got those same five tines buried just below his tail.

The bull went to the house. The boss was not proud when he saw his herd bull wearing a pitchfork, but the cowboy didn't give a rip whether the boss was proud or not. He had followed orders and had not shed any of his own blood.

Another fellow I knew up in Beaver County was calving out some two-year old heifers. He had five of them in a little trap behind the house, and one evening he tried to drive them into the corral for the night. Four of them went in, but the fifth one, who was as round as a whiskey keg, went up to the gate, sniffed, and ran back into the pasture.

This was repeated four or five times, until the cowboy was grinding his teeth in silent anger. A young buck would have roped the heifer, but she would have sulled, and with darkness coming on, the cowboy would have found himself in a mess. At the very best, he would have been late for supper. At the worst, he might have gone into one of those screaming fits that can produce a broken hand.

This cowboy was too wise for that. He parked his horse and climbed into his pickup. He got behind the heifer and honked and roared the engine. They made several laps around the trap, and when the heifer still wouldn't go through the gate, he rammed her, knocked her to the ground, and ran over her with the front and back wheels.

It would probably be a mistake to recommend this as a general management technique, but this time it worked. Not only did the heifer survive, she wasn't even hurt. She jumped up and ran straight to the corral, and several days later she delivered a healthy calf.

A cowboy never outgrows his temper. By the time he's old enough to work around livestock without getting mad, he's entirely too old for the job. But there's a time in his life when he leaves the follies of youth behind and learns to give his anger a more mature expression.

I'm proud to report that, seven years after he broke his toe on Macho, High Loper is showing a few signs of maturity. Last week he was trying to load a horned cow into the trailer. They had a dispute, and before long the old cow had Loper pinned against the corral fence.

Did he blow his top? Did he start throwing punches and karate kicks? Did he bellow and curse? No sir. He used reason and persuasion: "Now darling, I can see that you're upset, but let's try to be mature about this. Back off and let's try again."

The hard-bitten cynics among us won't believe it, but the old cow seemed to understand, and she responded to Loper's calm, reasonable appeal. She backed off and let him go. He thanked her and said it was always better to talk things over than to have childish displays of anger.

While she was thinking this over, he stepped outside the corral and came back with a seven-foot

bodark post. "Now get the hell in the trailer," he said.
She snorted and charged, and he knocked her to her
knees with the post.

Which just goes to prove that you can catch more
flies with sugar, but you can load more cows with a
bodark post.

Diary of a Bronc

May 1: Casey's my name, being an outlaw is my game. I'm five years old and never been rode. First man that tries me is gonna get throwed.

My momma ate dynamite and washed it down with gasoline. My old man ate pitchforks and rattlesnakes and barbed wire. He never walked around a tree. He'd kick it down and stomp on it. One time he got struck by lightning. The lightning bolt broke into seven pieces, and you can still see them lying out in the pasture.

I'm a bad dude, fellers, so give me room. The world owes me a living and I intend to collect. If I kill a couple of men along the way, it'll just be icing on my cake.

I want to hit the rodeo circuit, see. That's the place for this boy: show business, the easy life. Work eight seconds a week, man, throw some little snuffdippin' cowboy through the fence, and then eat prairie hay the rest of the time.

But, hey baby, I'm stuck out here on a nickel and dime cattle ranch in Texas. Ain't no bright lights around here. Ain't no excitement. The company's dull. My public's waiting for me up in Cheyenne. Got to get out of this place.

May 4: Man, these horses I have to live with around here are old and tired and corny. Like their idea of excitement is biting each other at the hay feeder. Ain't that wild? Ain't that western? What a bunch of scrubs.

Yesterday, old fat-boy Happy took a bite out of the Shetland and ran him around the corral. Thought he was pretty tough. I said, "Say, hoss, try that little action on me."

Heh, he tried it. If he hadn't weighed 1200, I'd have kicked him clean through the calf shed. Then that little Cookie mare came along, had her ears pinned down, trying to look mean. I cleaned house on her and said, "Okay, who's next?"

That's when old Popeye came up. He's, ahem, the elder statesman of the horse pasture. He'll weigh 1300, but he don't fight. Like he's above that childish stuff. He's ate up with religion.

"Casey," he said, "You're causing a lot of trouble around here."

And I said, "You got it right, Pops, only I ain't really got cranked up yet. When I do, yall better hunt a hole."

"One of these days you're going to come to grief."

"You gonna do it?"

"I might play a small part in it."

Man, I laughed in his face. "You handle the preachin', Pops, and I'll take care of the outlaw stuff, okay?"

The old fool just walked away. What could he say?

May 5: Life's getting exciting. The cowboys think it's time I was broke to a saddle. This morning they tried to catch me. That was a scream. Like they tried to slip up and put a halter on me, talking that "whoa, boy, easy bronc" stuff.

They got me in a corner, see, and thought they had me licked. Heh. I took the top two boards out of the corral fence and went on my way. Next time, I'll flatten the whole corral and stomp on it.

May 6: They got a rope halter on me. Ran me into a chute before I could really get my destructive trip going. Ah, who cares? A halter don't mean nuthin' to me. I'll just break it.

May 7: Didn't I say I'd break that halter? They tied me to a post, see, and I just went back on the rope and, bingo, no more halter. Kind of wish it hadn't broke. Had my heart set on jerking that post out of the ground.

May 8: These cowboys don't give up. They put a heavy nylon halter on me and they've got some kind of new rig on the snubbing post. They tied an inner tube to the post and they're fixing to tie me to the inner tube. That's cool. I'd just as soon tear up an inner tube as anything else.

Later: Inner tubes don't tear up so easy. I fought that thing for an hour and a half and I'm so tired I can hardly move. That's okay, it's all going according to my plan. Tomorrow I'm gonna give them total de-struction: post, inner tube, ropes, halter, corrals,

10

barns, the whole son of a buck. When I get done, man, we gonna have a big pile of toothpicks up here.

May 9: I ain't never been treated like *this* before. They stuck me on that danged inner tube and sacked me out till the world looked level. High Loper had a saddle blanket and Slim used his vest, and fellers, they worked me over. I gave it my best shot, but I got a feeling that I lost.

Okay, I've played around long enough. Tomorrow: total, absolute, utter destruction. Cowboys too.

May 10: Maybe tomorrow.

May 11: I got a funny feeling about this deal. That inner tube has wore me plumb out. The harder I pull back on it, the harder it slings me into the post. It could be a losing proposition.

May 12: Ha! They throwed a saddle on Preacher Popeye and clipped a lead rope onto my halter. They think Popeye's going to take me out into the pasture for a little stroll.

Well, hey, I got news for them. They beat me on the inner tube, but when they put me one-on-one against another horse, man, we gonna have some violence and bloodshed. I got a few tricks saved up for Popeye.

Later: Pops is stouter than you might think.

Later: I guess you might say that I'm halter broke. Slim snubbed me up to Popeye. I went back on the rope and fought like a wildcat. Figured I could jerk Pops off his feet.

Pops jerked *me* off *my* feet, out of my tracks, damned near out of my skin, and hauled me around the pasture like I was nothing but a smoked ham on a piece of string.

I fought him for a hundred yards, man, and decided that religion didn't hurt him none in the stouts department. I got whiplash all the way from my nose to the tip of my tail. May have to change my strategy.

May 13: Say, baby, what is this? Did I hear High Loper say that he's gonna climb on my back today? No way is that dude gonna climb on *my* back, cause my momma ate dynamite and washed it down with . . . "

Later: He did it.

May 14: He did it again. These guys don't play fair. They won't fight me when I'm fresh and full of vinegar. They put me on that inner tube, and then they hook me up to Pops and let him drag me around the pasture until I'm tired. By the time they start climbing into the saddle, I'm bushed, man, pooped. It ain't fair.

May 15: I'm beat. I surrender. They're winning.

May 16: Actually, it ain't so bad. Today I learned a little bit about neck reining. I've learned how to stop and go and back up on command. I hate to admit it, but I'm kind of proud of myself.

May 17: Loper and I made our first solo trip out in the pasture. I did a good job, I tried hard. I think Loper was proud of me.

May 20: We worked cattle today for the first time. Know what? I'm good at this, I really am, and derned if I don't kind of enjoy it.

June 2: I went to my first roundup today. I wasn't the star of the show, but I held my territory and did my job. I've noticed that the other horses are nicer to me now. They treat me with respect.

July 15: I guess I'll never make it to the Cheyenne rodeo, but I've sort of lost my desire for the high life.

I've got a good job here, friends, a nice place to live. Maybe that's enough.

August 15: We've got a new colt in the herd. Name's Chief, thinks he's hot stuff, says they're never going to break *him* to ride.

I had a little talk with him. I said, "You see that big horse over there? His name's Popeye, and he's *mucho caballo.* When the time comes, he'll make a Christian out of you."

The kid laughed in my face, called me an old duffer. These danged kids. They've got no respect for their elders. You can't tell them anything. I think this younger generation is going to hell in a bucket.

Roping Fools

Years ago, Will Rogers made a classic movie called "Roping Fool." I've never seen it but I read about it in Frank Dean's book, *Will Rogers' Rope Tricks.*

I glanced through the book one day after lunch. It was lying around the ranch house and I picked it up. High Loper, my cowboy partner, had ordered it from *The Western Horseman.*

The first thing I noticed was that the pages had little water stains on them. The stains got bigger toward the end of the book. High Loper was snoring away on his cot, catching a few winks before we hit the saddles again. I kicked him awake.

"Hey, what happened to your new book? It's got water stains on it."

He cracked one eye. It rolled around like a snooker ball in the corner pocket, then focused on me. "Have you read it yet?" I said no. "Read it. You'll see."

I started reading and couldn't quit. I missed my nap, and by the time I reached the end, I was weeping. That's where the water stains had come from: High Loper's tears.

We pulled on our coats and staggered out into the Panhandle cold, through the yard gate and past Loper's roping dummy. It had a busted leg where Loper had run over it with his pickup. We've had several dummies go lame that way.

Loper picked up his rope and built a loop. "Want to play a quick game of Horse?" He'd beat me the day before with a hoolihan from the left side. The hoolihan ain't my long suit.

"Nope. I've decided that roping's a vice and I'm going to give it up. I'm going to cut my rope into five pieces and throw it in the dump. I never want to see another rope."

He pitched his loop on the dummy's head and dallied in the air. "Was it the Will Rogers book?" I said it was. "I know how you feel."

We walked down to the corral. The wind was kicking up dust and sand. "You know, Loper, I always had a warm feeling about Will Rogers until I read that book."

"Me too."

"I thought he was one of us, just a common cowboy, a good old boy."

"Yeah, and a humorist. But that book wasn't funny."

"No sir. I wish you hadn't ordered it."

"Me too. It was a mistake."

I opened the saddle shed door and went inside, stumbled over the cat and kicked a can of Neat's foot oil. "Out of the way, cat. Hey, where's my bridle?

Where's my saddle? Somebody stole all my riggin'!"

Loper was leaning against the side of the door, picking his teeth. "It's on your horse. He's in the side lot where you left him."

"Oh. I guess my mind was somewhere else."

"Will Rogers?"

"Yeah, Will Rogers, dang him. I never dreamed he was such a smart aleck."

"They always said he was America's ambassador of good will."

"That's what they said." I took a bite off my plug of Bloodhound. "You know what really made me sick in that book? The picture where he threw an ocean wave that went around the back of a horse, came around the other side, and throat-latched him. And the horse was running."

Loper nodded. "How about the one where he threw three ropes and caught the head, forefeet, and the rider?"

"Yeah, and the one where he caught the head and forefeet in one loop."

"And roped a mouse with a piece of string."

"Don't say any more, I can't stand it. Loper, that book just broke my heart. Think of all the hours and years we've spent practicing on the dummy and roping out in the pasture, and all we can do is catch heads and heels."

"And sometimes we miss at that."

"I used to think I was a roper. I was a happy, normal cowboy who could strut around town and grin at all the people who didn't know a hock shot from a horn string. I was proud, I was content. I didn't want to be president of General Motors, just a good honest one-loop cowboy. Then you had to go and buy that danged Will Rogers book."

High Loper squinted against a blast of dust. "It's an awful feeling, being humble. I guess we ain't used to it."

"How can we ever hold our heads up again? How can we ever swing another loop, knowing all the things we can't do with it? I tell you, Loper, I'm a sick man. I need to go home and go to bed."

"Boss wouldn't be too proud if you did. I don't think he'd understand." We was quiet for a minute or two, each of us lost in our own sorrow. Then Loper cocked his head. "Say, do you reckon a man—I mean a normal man like me and you—could ever learn to rope a mouse with a piece of string?"

"I don't know. We've got plenty of practice stock in the feed barn, but they're awful quick to run."

The cat was rubbing up against Loper's leg. "Well, do you reckon a man could ever learn to rope a cat with a pigging string?"

I looked at him. He had a big grin on his face. "A man sure might." We ran to our horses in the side lot and jerked down our pigging strings. We loaded up and went looking for Pete. "Here kitty, kitty, kitty, nice kitty, here kitty."

The fool came, purring and rubbing up against the corner of the saddle shed. Loper got there first, swung, and let her rip. It went straight to the mark but old Pete hissed and ran through the loop.

Pete took off running and I was right behind him, chaps a-flapping and spurs a-jingling. High Loper was behind me, loading up for another shot.

We chased the son of a gun through the front lot, through the sick pen, out into the horse pasture, through a barbed wire fence, and out in front of the corrals. We blasted away but couldn't get him caught.

Then High Loper nailed him and we both let out cowboy yells, while Petie Pie squirmed and hissed. "Heel him!" said Loper.

I didn't know whether you could heel a cat or not, but I moved in for a throw. I had just laid down a beautiful trap when I heard a voice behind me.

"You boys having a good time?"

It was the boss. He was leaning up against the corral fence, had his arms crossed and was kind of tapping his toe. He'd snuck up on us and seen the whole thing.

He cleared his throat. "If you boys can work it into your schedule, I'd like to get those steers gathered off Cottonwood Creek. But if you're too busy . . . "

"No, no, we can . . . " Loper un-noosed the cat and rolled up his string. "We just . . . "

"You see," I said, "we read this . . . "

There are some things you just can't explain to the boss. We got ahorseback and headed for Cottonwood Creek. When we were alone, we looked at each other and grinned.

"I feel better," said Loper.

"Me too. Ain't it great to be a roping fool?"

"Will Rogers is okay."

Keeping Tally

In my book, *Panhandle Cowboy*, I made the observation that the primary disadvantage of cattle is that they are alive.

People who aren't involved in the cattle business might not understand this, but any cowboy who has put in some time on the lone prair-ee will know what I mean.

Not only do live animals insist on eating and drinking every day, but if you keep five hundred or a thousand of the little rascals around, there comes a time when you have to count them.

In an ordinary business venture, this is called inventory, and it's fairly simple. You count the boxes of soap on the shelf and write the number down on a piece of paper.

In the cattle business, it's called keeping tally and it ain't so simple, because cow brutes don't sit on a shelf. In fact, they rarely sit anywhere. They walk, run, scatter, hide, and jump fences, and before you can count them, you have to find them.

Once you've got them gathered, it ought to be a simple matter to count them, but somehow it's not. They mill and squirm. Two blacks standing side by side appear as one. A small steer standing behind a big steer is invisible. It's nothing unusual for two men to count the same bunch of cattle four or five times before they can agree on the tally.

When I first started out in this business, a rancher told me that the best way to count cattle was to count the legs and divide by four. Another man told me to count the legs and divide by 3.5. It didn't take me long to figure out that this was a standard joke in the profession. Every experienced cowboy knows that you count the ears and divide by three.

Counting a large number of cattle is difficult enough when you do it alone and without distractions, but when you have a dude riding with you, it becomes impossible. Let's say you have two hundred steers on the books and you want to check the tally to make sure they're all present and accounted for. And you take your friend with you.

You drive them into a corner and stir them around until they start trotting down the fence in single file. When they leave the herd in ones and twos, you can get a good reliable count.

But your friend doesn't understand what's going on and he keeps right on talking.

"51, 52, 53 . . . "

"These cows sure are pretty."

"Thanks, 54, 55, 56 . . . "

"When do they have their babies?"

"57, 58, steers don't, 59, 60, usually calve out, 61, 62, 63, till late spring, 64, 65 . . . "

"Huh. What's the matter with that one?"

"66, 67, 68, pinkeye."

"That one's limping."

"69, 70, foot-rot, 71, 72 . . . "

"What about that one?"

"73, 74, 75, shut up, 76, 77 . . . "

There is a minute of quiet. Then, "What do you think Reagan is going to do about inflation?"

"191, 192, 193, beats me."

"I sure hope he can get it stopped."

"194, 195, uh huh, 196 . . . "

"Oh, my gosh, look at that, will you!"

In spite of yourself, you turn away from the cattle. "What?"

"A big old jackrabbit!"

Sure enough, it's a big old jackrabbit, and you've lost your count. You have it all to do over again, but this time you send your friend off on a mission—to find a red billygoat in the far corner of the pasture.

Every cowboy has his own way of counting cattle, and if the conditions aren't just right, he doesn't feel good about his count. I prefer to have the cattle pass by on the right side of my horse because I point my right hand at every animal as I count him.

If they pass me on the left, I have to point across my body, which just doesn't seem to work out. You'd think that a normal, fairly coordinated cowboy could count as well with his left hand as with his right, but that's not the case with me. I never trust a lefthanded count.

There's another quirk about my counting method that I don't understand. Not only do I have to point with my right hand, I have to take the glove off that hand as well. What does a glove have to do with a good count? I don't know, but there you are.

I've known other cowboys who counted by twos or threes and some who bobbed their heads instead of pointed their fingers. The worst kind of man to work with is one who counts out loud. No matter how hard you try to ignore his muttering, it gets into your ears and then soaks into your brain. Before long, all you can think about is telling him to shut his yap, and you lose your count.

There is also the kind of man—usually a rookie on the crew but not always—who wants to be the first to get the count. He rarely comes up with the correct number, but that doesn't seem to bother him as long as he's the first one through. He slops through his count and then yells out, "I got a hundred and ninety-seven! What did you get?"

Unless you possess iron discipline and tremendous powers of concentration, this fellow will blow your count every time.

If you are employed on a ranch that runs a large number of cattle, you can't remember the tally in all the pastures, so you have to keep your numbers in a tally book. On our outfit, which has cattle scattered all over the country in fifteen or twenty pastures, we don't dare leave headquarters without a tally book.

Mine is a small black book that fits into my shirt pocket. This works fine in the summer when I wear shirts with button-down flaps on the pockets. Unfortunately, my flannel shirts, which I wear all winter long, don't have flaps, so any time I shuck off my vest, I have to start chasing my tally book.

There is a little ritual I go through every morning when I hook up the stock trailer. I bend over to crank

the trailer down on the hitch ball. My tally book falls out of my pocket. I bend over to pick it up and my chewing tobacco falls out. I curse and bend over to get the chewing tobacco and my matches fall out. I bellow, pick up the matches, and my ballpoint pen falls out.

When I've emptied out both shirt pockets, then I can get on with the rest of the day's work.

I've also planted a few tally books out in the pasture. This usually happens when an outlaw steer breaks from the herd and High Loper and I are horse-racing to see who gets first loop. When you're up in the stirrups, swinging a hungry noose, grinning that wicked cowboy grin, and your tally book sprouts wings, it just breaks your heart.

If you don't quit the chase, you lose your tally book and therefore your brains. But if you stop to get it, you know that High Loper won't be loose-herding the roping stock and waiting for you to go get ahorse-back again. He'd beat his own grandmother out of a pasture shot. In fact, I think he'd *rope* his own grand-mother if she ever got out of the yard.

So you stop and go back for the tally book. Just as you bend down to pick it up, you hear Loper let out a squall. There's only two things that can make him squall like that: either he got his finger caught in the dally or else he made a mighty pretty one-looper. But either way, he's beat you out of a shot. All because of a derned tally book.

Which just goes to prove what I said at the begin-ning, that the cow business would be a bunch easier if the product wasn't alive, if you could stack it up on the shelf like boxes of soap and take a tally once a year. But come to think of it, that would sure cut down on the pasture roping, so maybe we'd better just leave things as they are.

Cattle Ain't Very Smart

When a young man chooses to go into the cowboy profession, there are many axioms and rules of bovine animal behavior that he must master.

He must learn that all breeds of cattle don't behave in exactly the same manner. All classes of cattle (bulls, heifers, cows, calves) have their own quirks and behavior patterns. The cattle in pasture A may behave differently from those across the fence in pasture B, and those in pasture B may not behave the same today as they did yesterday, depending on the temperature and weather conditions.

Indeed, there are so many rules of cow psychology and so many exceptions to rules, so many opinions and counter-opinions, that a guy could easily get the feeling that there are no constants at all and that cattle are wholly unpredictable.

That's getting close to the truth, but it's not quite

right. Over the years I've learned one rule that you can tie onto hard and fast. If you didn't know anything else about cattle, this rule would tell you about as much about cattle as any one rule could.

The rule: you should never underestimate the stupidity of a cow brute.

Reading J. Frank Dobie, I get the impression that he thought the old-time Longhorn cattle had some brains and good sense. I wouldn't dare question Mr. Dobie's judgment on this matter, so I have to believe that something very bad has happened to cattle since he was gathering stories forty or fifty years ago.

Because the cattle I handle every day, winter, spring, summer, and fall, show signs of severe mental retardation. And steers may be the worst of all. God, they're dumb.

Last winter me and High Loper had to nursemaid a bunch of steers on a patch of wheat up on the Texas-Oklahoma state line. We turned them out in November, and when we let them out of the stock trailers, we pointed them right straight at the water tanks on the north end, so they couldn't possibly miss the point: "Boys, this here is water, and you'll need to take a drink of it every day."

So what did they do? For the next three days they stood bunched up on the south fence, bawling for water. If we'd put the tanks on the south end, they would have gone to the north end to bawl.

For the first week they were on that place, we had to haul our horses twenty-five miles up to the state line and drive the little dummies to water, without which they would have perished.

Along in January the weather turned foul. The steers on this place didn't have any natural protection from the wind-driven cold, and me and Loper began to feel sorry for them. We spent one whole afternoon planting posts in the ground and building them a nice little windbreak.

A few days later, a storm blew in out of the northwest: snow, sleet, wind, the whole nine yards. Just to be on the safe side, we hauled our horses up to the state line and checked on our retardos. Sure enough, there they were on the south fence again, humped up like a bunch of camels, shivering, bawling, and growing icicles on their noses.

We had to drive them into the storm and hold them for half an hour behind the windbreak. By the time we left, a small miracle had occurred: those fifty steers had figured out that it's warmer behind a windbreak than in front of it or beside it or even down on the south fence.

Last summer we got another example of steer stupidity. We had a set of fresh-bought steers in the home pasture. We rode them every day to make sure they didn't come down sick or find some other way of committing suicide.

One day High Loper came up short a steer. He rode and he looked, and he looked and he rode, and he was still short one steer. Days passed. We checked the adjoining pastures. No steer.

About a week later, Loper was riding along the creek and found him. This little genius had somehow managed to get his head caught between two willow trees that were about a foot apart. Instead of turning his head sideways, which is how he had gotten in there, he pulled straight back and fought and struggled and tried to pull the trees down, which didn't work.

By the time Loper found him, he was in poor

condition. His head was sitting in the fork of the trees, and the rest of him, what the coyotes had left, was scattered over half an acre.

A couple of years ago, when I was working on a ranch in the Oklahoma Panhandle, I was out on my daily feed run when I spotted a critter on a far hill. He was off by himself and he had a funny way of walking. And, at a distance, it appeared to me that he didn't have a head, which seemed odd.

I drove across the sandhills and took a closer look. This brainless wonder (again, a steer) had found a five gallon bucket lying out in the pasture, stuck his head into it, and started wearing it. He was quite blind, was staggering around in search of food and water, and I would imagine that his ears were ringing. Had he lowered his head just a few inches, the bucket would have fallen off, but that was beyond his mental capacity.

I walked up to him and pulled it off. If I hadn't chanced upon him, he would have died a miserable death.

Steers are well known for their uncanny ability to get into things they can't get out of. About a month ago I spent an afternoon riding through several bunches of steers on wheat pasture. On the Anderson place, we had a hundred and fifty-nine steers. I rode through them, made a careful count, and found only a hundred fifty-eight.

I rode through them again, two more times, to check my count, until I was satisfied that the steer was indeed missing. I rode back to my pickup and trailer, wondering where I should start looking.

There was a junkyard on this place, between the water tanks and the pasture, and the steers had to pass

through it on their way to and from water. It was a patch of about ten acres where the owner of the land stored articles that were not often used but were too good to throw away.

There were several big piles of cedar posts, rolls of barbed wire, dead trees, stacks of lumber, farm machinery, an old truck, and several junk cars. I had already ridden through the junkyard and had checked it out, but on a hunch I decided to walk it out afoot.

I walked along, leading my mare. I looked everywhere and saw nothing of the missing steer. I had given up and was on my way to the trailer when I heard a sound behind me. I turned around and looked.

There, fifty feet from where I stood, a Hereford steer was staring at me. I could just see the top of his head. He was sitting behind the wheel of a wrecked Ford Mustang.

There was no door on the driver's side of the car, and the steer had walked inside. Once there, it had not occurred to him that by merely walking backward three or four steps, he could be outside again with his friends. So he had camped out inside the car for three or four days, lost thirty or forty pounds of weight, and flirted with death.

You can't help wondering what it is that makes a steer think that he needs to get inside a car, or stick his head into a grease bucket, or slip his head between two trees.

It's one of those mysteries of life that has no good answer. All the cowboy can do is shake his head and repeat Rule Number One: Never underestimate the stupidity of a cow brute.

My New Grass Rope

By the time I came of age and learned how to rope, the old grass rope had just about passed into history. And for good reason. The nylon was a better tool. It was stronger, it held its shape better in all kinds of weather, and you didn't have to wax it or soak it in the stock tank to get the figure-eights out of it.

I ran into a few old-timers who still packed a grass rope, usually tied to an old bronc saddle with a high cantle and a big swell and tiny horn. You could tell at a distance that it was a grass rope because it appeared that it was still squirming, like a snake with its head cut off.

One day in 1979 I was in Stockman's Supply, killing time and messing with a new shipment of ropes they had just gotten in. I played around with a couple of nylons and a poly, and then I saw this grass rope hanging on a peg. It was orange in color and about twenty-five feet long. The guy who ran the store told me that this style of rope was a favorite with some calf ropers.

I'd never used a grass rope, so I took it down and swung it around several times. It sure didn't have the same feel as my medium lay nylon. It was a heavy rope, yet limp. The price was fifteen bucks.

I just happened to have fifteen bucks in my pocket. I don't remember why. It was unusual for me to be walking around with such a big wad of cash in my jeans.

One reason I didn't carry much cash was that by the time the bill collectors got through with me, I was usually down to Coke and chew change, just enough to make a jingle in my pocket.

The other reason I didn't carry much money was that I had a bad habit of taking it into Stockman's and blowing it on a new catch rope. I know that a man can't use but one rope at a time, but when an ordinary mortal cowboy wanders into Stockman's and gets in the middle of all those new ropes, something happens to his better judgment.

As old Sandy Hagar used to say, "If you put a dollar bill in one pocket and a wildcat in the other, it's hard to predict which one will get out first." With me in Stockman's a wildcat wouldn't have a chance.

I bought the derned rope and got out of there before I could stray over into the boot section. Buying ropes is bad enough. Craving new boots is plumb dangerous.

When I got down to the ranch, I went straight to the roping dummy and started throwing my new grass rope. At first it felt too heavy, and I didn't care for the action of the loop when it went around the head. But I kept playing with it, and after a while I decided that it was all right. I could see why calf ropers liked this kind of rope, because if you put the loop in the right place, it didn't walk around. It stayed there.

I tied it onto my horn string and hung my nylon on the wall. Next time I got into an argument with a steer, I'd give her a test under pasture conditions and see how she worked.

Several days later I was riding through a bunch of new steers in the home pasture. It was a gray, cloudy day, and there was a little nip in the wind. I came up one short on my count and started prowling the holes and hollows along the creek, looking for a sick one.

I found him on the east end of the pasture, over by Parnell's water gap. He was off by himself, standing in creek water up to his knees, a sign that he had a fever. His ears were drooped and his eyes had a sad, hollow look that reminded me of what I see in the mirror some mornings.

I bellered at him and gave him a few choice words, but he didn't want to leave the water. I rode in and stirred him out. Just in case he didn't want to leave, I had my new grass rope loaded.

I got behind him and drove him toward the corral. I could tell he didn't want to go because he kept looking toward the creek and trying to break back. As sick as he was, I sure didn't want him to get back into the water.

We were within about two hundred yards of the pens when he made a run for the creek, and this time I couldn't turn him. He started running down the north bank, and I followed him. He'd had his chance to go peacefully, and he was fixing to meet the long arm of the law—my new grass rope.

The north bank was steep at this point, and the creek was narrow and deep. There was just enough room on that high bank for a horse to walk, and the farther we went, the narrower the path became. Finally the old steer ran out of path. There was a high bank on the right and a four-foot drop into the water on the left.

I crowded him and he tried to crawl the bank. He couldn't quite make it and fell into the water. His head went under and he came up swimming. That was a pretty deep hole.

"Serves you right, you old fool," I told him.

Now I had to figure a way to get myself out. There wasn't enough room to turn my mare. So I started backing her out. Her left rear hoof broke off a piece of the bank and we went over backwards into the hole. I had just enough time to kick out of the stirrups before we hit the water with a big kersplash.

It was a Baptist kind of spill (total immersion) and I went in deep enough to float my Resistol. I got everything gathered up and staggered out on the south bank. I had gone in weighing a hundred and seventy pounds and came out weighing about two-forty.

I was soaked and cold, but my mainest problem was that my high-topped Noconas were filled with water. I'd never been able to get them off without a boot jack. And I sure couldn't get them off now, with a wet sock and suction and all. So I laid down on my back and raised my feet over my head and let the water drain down my legs. That cold water sure said howdy to my private parts.

I climbed back on my mare, poked her with the spurs, and went after the steer. After he'd gotten me

baptized, I was going to stick a rope on him whether he needed it or not. I found him about fifty yards down the creek. I still had my loop built.

But I noticed that something was different. My new grass rope had changed. The loop weighed about five pounds and it felt like a chunk of half-inch cable. If a man needed to rope anything smaller than a locomotive, he probably wouldn't get his slack pulled up in time to make a catch. And heaving the derned thing, he'd run some risk of throwing his shoulder out of socket.

The steer got off easy. I had to pen him in the conventional manner, and then I ran to the house for dry clothes.

Well, I still hadn't tested out my new rope, and there was no way I could use it until it dried out and softened up. I left it behind the seat of the pickup and figured I'd check it in a week or so.

Several days later, my boss tried to pull a five-section harrow through a gate that was about four harrow-sections wide. To get it through, he had to pull one end back and the other end forward, and then take it longways through the gate.

We usually carried an old junk rope behind the seat of the pickup, so he reached back there and pulled it out. He hooked it onto the harrow and pulled it around with the pickup. It worked fine, except that the old junk rope broke in half. And it wasn't a junk rope. It was my new grass rope, which didn't look so new after I'd taken it swimming.

The boss regretted his mistake and paid me fifteen bucks for a new rope, but the bill collectors got it before I could make it back down to Stockman's.

Today, a year and a half after I bought it, my new

grass rope is hanging on a nail in the saddle shed. It has dried out and regained its nice shape, but it's only ten feet long and a little frayed on the bitter end.

I still haven't roped any livestock with a grass rope, and I guess I never will. But it hasn't been a total loss and I've learned a few things about grass ropes: don't use them to pull farm machinery and don't take them into the bathtub with you.

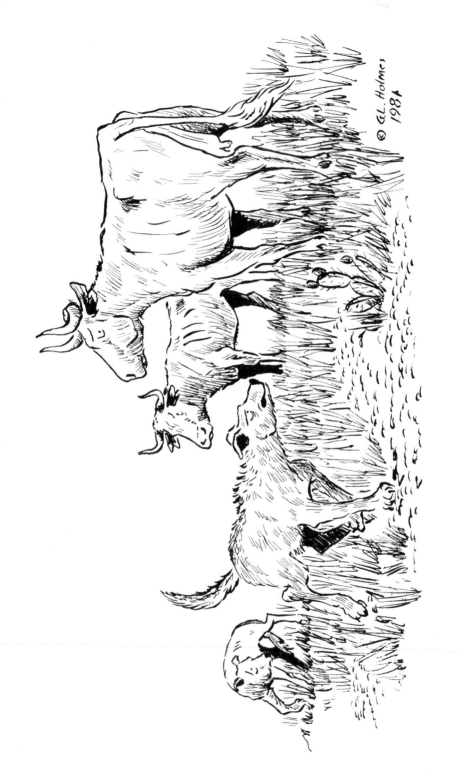

Confessions of a Cowdog

August 15: My name's Hank. I'm a cowdog on a ranch in Texas. I never heard of a cowdog keeping a diary, but I'm going to give it a try.

My ma came from good stock. They were Australians, back to who laid the chunk, and they were all good with cattle. Ma used to say that Uncle Beanie was the best cowdog in South Texas.

But she fell in with a bad crowd when she was young, and that's where she met my old man. She used to tell me about him: "He was a good bloke, but just a wee bit south of worthless."

I asked her what it was that attracted her to him. She got a far-off look in her eyes and sighed. "We were both young and foolish. He was a dashing rogue. Hank, that daddy of yours could pee on more tires than any dog in Texas." That always stuck with me, kind of gave me a standard to aim for.

41

August 25: It was terrible hot today. This long hair makes me awfully uncomfortable. Me and Drover spent most of the morning shaded up beneath the gas tanks. I didn't think I had enough energy to move— until Pete came along.

Pete's the barn cat around here. I don't like him. I don't like his looks. I don't like his attitude. I don't like cats in general. I whipped him and ran him up a tree.

That got me all hot and worked up, so I went up to the septic tank. It overflows and there's always a nice cool puddle of water there. I plopped down in it. Oh, it felt good. I rolled around and kicked all four legs in the air. When I got out, I felt like a million.

I trotted down to the house, just as Slim and High Loper were coming out the yard gate. I trotted up to say howdy. I rubbed up against Loper's leg and gave myself a good shake. I guess I hit him with some mud and water. Made him mad.

"Git outa here, Dang it!" He's a funny guy, gets mad at little things. When he's in a good humor, he calls me Hank. When he's mad, he calls me Dang it. When he's really mad, he calls me other things. I answer to anything.

September 1: It was cloudy and cool today. Me and Drover were sleeping down at the corrals. Drover's my running buddy, a small, short-haired white dog. He's got no cow sense at all, just doesn't understand the business. I think he's scared of cattle.

Well, I was sleeping, don't you see, and Drover woke me up. "Hank, get up, boy, there's cattle coming this way, a whole herd of them, coming in like elephants!"

I'm in charge of ranch security. I don't allow cattle up around the place. I came out of a dead sleep and jumped to my feet.

42

We went ripping out of the corral, me in the lead and Drover bringing up the rear. He was right about the cattle. It was a by-gosh invasion, fifty, sixty head of stock.

I went straight to the lead cow. She was a horned wench, and had an evil temper to boot. She dropped her head and started throwing hooks at me. Out in the pasture, maybe I would have backed away. But not this time. I was protecting the ranch (did I mention that I'm in charge of ranch security?), and I was prepared to give my life if necessary.

She rolled me once with them big horns, which kind of inflamed me, don't you see, and I put the old Australian fang-lock on her nose. Ma would have been proud of me. In seconds, I had that north-bound herd going south. Drover was right behind me, cheering me on. "Git 'em, Hankie, sick 'em, boy!"

I sicked 'em, all right, but come to find out, Slim and High Loper were trying to pen them in the corral. How was I supposed to know? Next thing I knew, High Loper was coming at me, swinging his rope and calling my name. "Dangit, git outa here!"

I got chased up to the yard. I don't know what happened to Drover. He just sort of disappeared when things went sour. He does that a lot.

September 15: Had a wild time last night. Me and Drover was sleeping by the yard gate. Along about midnight, he woke me up.

"Hear that?" he whispered. I listened and heard it. Coyotes, and they were close. "Let's run 'em off."

"You think we should?" I was still half-asleep.

"Heck yes. This is our ranch, ain't it?"

"Good point. But I don't want any rough stuff. Those guys are thugs."

We loped up the hill until we could see a coyote standing in the road, a skinny, scruffy-looking little villain. I barked at him and told him to scram, we didn't allow no coyote trash around our ranch. He told me to drop dead.

I was ready to leave it at that, but Drover thought we had a responsibility to the ranch. "Let's give him a whipping. There's two of us and only one of him."

I counted, and sure enough, we had him outnumbered two to one. "Well, all right, if you think we should."

He thought we should. So I swaggered out and jumped the coyote. I throwed him to the ground while Drover nipped at his tail.

I sure was surprised when that little coyote's uncles and cousins and big brothers showed up. All at once I was in the midst of a coyote family reunion. Man alive, they was biting me in places I'd never been bit before.

"Come on, Drover!" I yelled. "Don't save anything back, boy, this is the real thing!"

Drover had disappeared. I managed to escape with everything but two pounds of hair and part of my left ear. An hour later, I found Drover, huddled up in the darkest, backest corner of the machine shed.

I was all set to whip the tar out of him, but he cried and begged and told me that, down deep, he was opposed to violence. How can you whip a dog that says that?

November 1: Got into trouble today. High Loper and Slim were doctoring sick cattle this morning, running them through the squeeze chute and giving them shots and pills and stuff.

Me and Drover were hanging around, watching. The cowboys went to dinner and left all the medicine beside the chute.

Drover went over and sniffed at a cardboard box full of big white pills. "You know what these are? Amino acid boluses. They're supposed to give energy to sick cattle. They're good for cowdogs too."

I walked over to the box and sniffed. "Smells good. But wouldn't the cowboys be mad if we ate 'em?"

"Oh, heck no. It says right there on the box that cowdogs are *supposed* to eat them."

I squinted at the box. "So it does."

I pulled one out and chewed on it. Say, that stuff was good. I went back for another one, and another one, and then I went back for seconds. It beat the heck out of that cheap co-op dog food.

Before long, the box was empty. When the cowboys came back from lunch, I was sunning myself beside the chute, full and happy and feeling good. I gave the boys a grin and wagged my tail.

High Loper stared at the empty box. "Where did those . . . " He looked at me. I must have had a few crumbs on my chops. "Why you worthless cur, that box cost twenty-one dollars!"

Huh? I looked around for Drover. He had disappeared. About then the rocks and sticks started flying, and I ran for my life.

I found Drover in the machine shed and I jumped right in the middle of him. He cried and begged but I didn't listen this time. My momma didn't raise no fool.

"Wait!" he cried. "If you won't whip me, I'll tell you a deep, dark, awful secret."

"Huh? An awful secret?"

"Yeah. Listen. It was all *Pete's* idea. He wanted to get us into trouble."

"Naw. No foolin'?"

He raised his right paw. "It's God's truth, Hankie."

"Why that sorry, no good for nuthin' cat! Come on, Drover, it's time to clean house."

I marched down to the saddle shed, caught Pete plumb by surprise, whupped him, re-whupped him, and ran him up a tree. Drover was behind me all the way, cheering me on.

"Git 'im, Hankie, git 'im!"

That was that. We went up for a roll in the sewer, and I said to Drover, "Boy, I can't believe Pete would try to pull a deal like that on us cowdogs. How dumb does he think we are?"

He shook his head. "Pretty dumb, Hank, pretty dumb."

Log of a Cowhorse

October 1: My name is Happy. I work on a cattle ranch in the Texas Panhandle. I'm a cowhorse.

I'm one of twelve horses on this outfit. An impartial judge of horseflesh would say that I'm the fastest, smartest, and handsomest horse on the ranch. What can I say? No matter how hard you try to blend in and get along with the other guys, if you're superior in every way, the word just seems to get out.

Oh, I have flaws. Surely I have flaws. Well, maybe I don't.

We've had fine grass in the horse pasture this summer. My sorrel coat shines like polished brass, and I'm up to a gorgeous 1200 pounds. I was admiring myself in the creek yesterday when that Shetland pony came along and muddied the water.

They call him Lightning. I call him Pipsqueak. He's a jealous, overbearing, insignificant little snot of a horse. I never miss a chance to bite him. That's all he's good for.

I have a pretty good life down here on Wolf Creek, though it would be better if the cowboys would leave me alone. They throw a saddle on me and make me work. They don't seem to understand that I have better things to do. Don't they realize who I am?

October 7: Had a norther last night and there's a nip in the air this morning. The grass is getting short and I seem to be hungry all the time.

About ten minutes ago, High Loper, one of the so-called cowboys on this outfit, stepped out of the feed barn and held up a rubber feed bucket. He looked out into the horse pasture and whistled at us. Pipsqueak headed for the corral in a run. Frisco and Calipso followed him.

Not me. I stayed where I was. Deuce and Popeye stayed with me, but they were looking toward the corral. Popeye said that he was hungry and sure could use some of that grain.

"It's just a trick," I told him. "Those cowboys think they can rattle a feed bucket and we'll come running in like that greedy little Shetland. As soon as we get into the corral, they're going to shut the gate and start slinging saddles on us. It's the oldest trick in the book."

Popeye kept looking toward the corral. "I sure could use some grub."

"Then go on," I told him. "But when they throw a cold saddle on you and put you to work, don't blame me." Popeye and Deuce started slinking away. "That's right, be a couple of chumps. But you won't see *me* in there. I've got better things to do."

They trotted off, then broke into a gallop. Old

plowhorse Popeye even managed to kick his heels up once or twice. I watched. Sure enough, High Loper sprinkled a few pieces of corn and barley into the trough, and Slim snuck around and shut the gate. Loper put a bridle on Popeye and led him to the saddle lot.

I told him. In this life, the fools get caught and saddled. Those of us in the elite have figured out the game and refuse to play. We have better things to do.

Later that day: It seems that High Loper was offended that I didn't fall for his fool's trick. He saddled Popeye and came out after me. I made a run up the

© G.L. Holmes

canyon but he cut me off. He was in a snit. He cursed at me and tried to rope me.

Did he actually believe he could rope me in the pasture? *Me*? I turned on my amazing speed and left his loop hanging in the air. However, I thought it prudent to run toward the corral. Give these cowboys enough time and enough throws, and they're just liable to slop one on.

I went to the corral, but it was by choice, not by force. I had already decided that a little ride across the ranch might prove interesting. When I got into the corral, I went straight over to Pipsqueak and took a hunk out of his withers, just to let him know where he stood around the place.

The little snot kicked me in the ribs. Well, I pinned back my ears and made another dive at him, and he kicked me in the shoulder. I guess that'll teach him.

That night: Derned ribs hurt all day. Pipsqueak's going to regret that.

Next day: Heh, heh. Nailed him at the waterhole this morning. He's got a bald spot on his rump now.

November 21: It started raining yesterday morning, rained all day and into the night. This morning around daylight it changed to snow.

A while ago, I overheard Calipso and Deuce talking. They were all humped up and shivering and complaining about the weather. I said, "Why are you complaining? As long as the weather stays lousy, the cowboys will leave us alone. They don't ride in bad weather, you know."

Calipso, who is half-Arabian and just a little snooty about it, said she would rather work than stand around in the cold. Deuce agreed, which I thought was funny because he's the laziest horse on the ranch.

At that moment Calipso raised her head and cocked her ears. I looked toward the corral and saw Slim, the tall skinny cowboy, riding toward us on Popeye.

"I thought you said they didn't work in bad weather," said Deuce.

I was astounded. Slim rounded us up and drove us into the corral. High Loper appeared with bridles and they led me and Calipso to the saddle lot. Loper threw a cold, clammy saddle on my back and jerked down the cinches.

They loaded me and Calipso into a wet, slimy stock trailer and hauled us up north to a wheat field. The wind was howling and little pellets of ice rattled on the roof of the trailer.

They opened the trailer gates and told me to unload. I took one look at the mud and slop outside and I said, "You can forget that, mates, I'm staying in here."

High Loper got a two-by-four out of the back of his pickup and I changed my mind. You never know until you try, I always say, and you can always back down.

I can't describe how ghastly it was, stepping out into that cold muck. I sank to my fetlocks and the mud oozed over my hooves. When High Loper climbed into the saddle, I was ready to buck.

On dry ground, he wouldn't have had a chance. I would have had him shucked off in three jumps. But when you can hardly pull your hooves out of the mud, it's hard to generate much thunder and lightning. High Loper was lucky this time, but I'll get him another day.

That night: I hate mud. I hope horse heaven is a desert.

December 2: Got my revenge on High Loper. We roped a steer this morning, and before Loper could dally up, I came to a sudden stop. He lost his rope. Boy, was he mad.

Later: Boy, was he mad. I have spur tracks on both shoulders. We had to chase the steer down to get the rope back. There may be better ways of getting revenge. I shall give this some thought.

December 8: More mud, more snow. Nose was running this morning.

December 9: Nose running worse, got a bad cough.

December 10: Cough worse. I feel lousy.

December 11: It's distemper. They're giving me shots. Too sick to work.

December 18: Feeling better now, but still weak. Haven't worked for a long time.

December 19: I'm getting bored.

December 20: I'm bored stiff. Why don't the cowboys ride me any more? Surely they must realize that Deuce can't take my place in the work string.

December 21: I'm fed up with standing around the pasture all day with brood mares and Pipsqueak. I have better things to do.

December 22: Enough is enough. High Loper opened the gate this morning and whistled. I ran all the way and was the first horse in. He saddled me up. We're going up to wheat pasture. Oh happy day!

That night: Worked hard, had a great day. I don't understand it. I always thought I hated work. Makes me wonder about the meaning of this life. All I can say is that work is bad, but the alternatives may be worse.

Cow Doctors

It seems that one of the natural by-products of a yearling operation is sick cattle. It doesn't matter how well you handle them or how many times you check them, a certain percentage of the little boogers are going to get sick.

Part of our job as cowboys is finding the sick ones in the pasture. We've studied the signs and the symptoms, and we sort of know what we're doing.

Bloaters are easy to spot. When you run onto a steer that's swollen up like a poisoned pup; when it appears that he's going to have twin calves; when you can see him half a mile away and can't decide whether he's one steer or three, you can figure he's a bloater.

Bad pinkeyes stand out from the bunch too. When you see one off by himself, walking around in circles, you begin to suspect pinkeye. When you ride up to him, and he walks right through your horse's legs, you're sure of the diagnosis.

In this type of case, you take immediate action. You put a choke hold on the saddle horn and try to get your horse under control. Then, if you're still ahorseback, you do something about the pinkeye. If you're not, then you might need to visit the chiropractor before you can work any miracles on the bad-eyed steer.

Steers with pneumonia generally fall into one of several categories. There are the droopers, the stumblers, the coughers, the wheezers, the dry-nosers, the snot-nosers, and the crazies.

There is one more pneumonia category that we don't like to discuss. These are called the deceased. They are easy to find and diagnose, and require very little care.

High Loper and I have found several of these and have made a study of them. Our data show that when an animal dies on Friday, lying on his side with his legs pointing north, he will still be dead on Saturday.

Steers with gut problems show another set of symptoms. They will be gant, lethargic, and, shall we say, dirty around the tail. Loading one of these critters into a stock trailer will test the mettle of a cowboy. A brave man will twist the tail, put his shoulder into the animal's rump, and do his job. Later, he will burn his clothes.

On this outfit, when a sick animal is brought in from the pasture, he goes to the sick pen. He is rushed to the squeeze chute and comes under the care of the two resident C.D.'s (Cow Doctors), me and High Loper. You'd think that this in itself would scare any sensible animal into good health, but it doesn't. We keep getting customers.

© G.L. Holmes

High Loper is the chief of staff. Before receiving his C.D. certificate, he underwent a rigorous training period, during which he talked to the local vet three times, read several articles, and studied the label directions on every bottle in the medicine shed.

In his spare time, he also took a correspondance course: Hide and Rendering 101. A good C.D. has to be realistic about these things.

Under Loper's administration, our sick pen runs smoothly and efficiently. Our sick animals receive the very best treatment available to modern veterinary science. In addition to the usual medication, they receive feed, water, air, and verbal abuse.

They receive verbal abuse because, in spite of our high ideals and dedication, we hate them. The moment they enter our sick pen, we greet them with snarls. The longer they stay, the more we despise them.

The ones we hate the least are the ones who have the courtesy and the common decency to get well after a four-day run of antibiotics. We can forgive these for getting sick. It wasn't their fault. They didn't start wheezing and dropping their ears just to torment us. They don't like us any better than we like them.

The ones we hate the most are the chronics. We give them four days' of antibiotics and they get worse. We switch them to spectinomycin and go to the trouble of giving it in the vein, and they get worse.

We give them sulfamethazine liquid. We give them Tylan and furacin. We give them amino acid boluses and wash them down with sixteen drench guns of water. We give them an electrolyte solution in the peritoneum, vitamin B, and ten cc's of that yellow stuff in the little bottle.

And they get worse.

Around our outfit, you hit the low point of the year about the middle of January. At eight o'clock in the morning, you walk down to the corrals. You're reasonably happy and content with the world.

The temperature is ten degrees. The wind is blowing. The ground is frozen. Every cow chip and horse biscuit has become a rock. You stumble through the alley on feet that are already growing numb.

You throw open the gate and enter the sick pen. There they are: ten sicks, four real sicks, and three chronics. The chronics lift their heads and stare at you with sunken eyes, as if to say, "I ain't gonna eat, I ain't gonna drink, I ain't gonna get well, but I ain't gonna die either, so get the pills ready, cowboy."

Your affection for these chronics diminishes every time they give you that greeting, and it seems to drop with the temperature.

Since a chronic won't trouble himself to drink from the stock tank, you have to give him water with a drench gun. We have hard water in the Panhandle. In January it becomes so hard that we have to chop it with an axe and melt it down on the branding heater.

It takes time. It takes time to fill the drench gun sixteen times, force open the animal's jaws, and squirt the water so far down his guzzle that he can't possibly spit it out, because if you don't, he will.

You spend twenty minutes on this chronic. When you've given him his water, every pill and every injection you can think of, you let him out of the chute. He staggers out, which always makes you proud, drags his carcass about ten steps, turns around, and faces you. And while you administer to the next chronic, he stares at you with that rebuking look of death.

High Loper has become so sensitive to this that

he will stop what he's doing and force the beast to look the other direction.

Chronics give every indication of being uncommonly stupid. What else can you conclude about an animal that won't eat or drink? But Loper and I have noted a certain cunning in these wretches. They seem to know when you've put fifty dollars' worth of medicine in them. It seems to activate a response in their autonomic nervous system. When the fifty-dollar mark is passed, they drop dead, but they won't do it for a penny less.

Loper and I have had some dark moments in the sick pen, but we try to look at the brighter side. As he pointed out one day, "Look at it this way. It could be worse. We could be working in a warm office, sitting in soft chairs, smoking good cigars, watching nubile secretaries pass by the door, and making fifty thousand a year."

At that moment we had to rush back to the sick pen and administer the rites of extreme unction to one of our animal friends, who had just hit the fifty dollar jackpot.

"You're right, Loper," I said. "This may not be the best job in the world, but it sure is the worst."

Sally May's Journal

July 8: My name is Sally May. I am High Loper's wife. We live on a ranch in the Texas Panhandle.

Our house is old and small, but I try to keep it nice. Yesterday morning I spent four hours sweeping and dusting and scrubbing the woodwork. I had let it go too long.

At noon, Loper and Slim came up for lunch. They had spent the morning sorting cattle in the corral. I can always tell when they have been working in the corral. The smell of the house changes when they walk in the door.

I had left the boot jack on the back step. I didn't want to be a nag, and I thought maybe this subtle hint would work.

I heard the yard gate slam. I heard their spurs jingling on the sidewalk. I heard them talking and laughing on the back step. I heard the door open. I heard their boots and spurs on my clean floor, and then I caught the smell.

They did not take their boots off. I pointed this out to Loper. He said they forgot.

July 9: They forgot to take their boots off again. I try to be patient with them, but patience has its limits. My husband is fond of telling stories that show what stubborn brutes his cattle are. Next time he does this, I shall bring him a mirror.

July 10: They did it again. Hints do not seem to work on cowboys. They came clomping into the kitchen with their boots and spurs on. I showed restraint and did not complain.

Oh, did I mention that the lunch burned while I was sweeping the dirt and manure? Yes, it did. What a pity. Loper and Slim love rare steaks. Alas, the steaks were charred. The potatoes burned, and somehow I over-salted them. The corn on the cob was awfully tough. After the meal, Slim did his hardest work of the year, prying corn husks out of his teeth.

July 11: My husband is catching on, I think. Last night we discussed the boot situation. He brought it up.

He said they don't like to take their boots off outside. They get stickers in their bare feet, and in the winter their boots get too cold. He thought it would be much easier if we had a utility room.

I told him this was an excellent idea. He agreed, but added that they are too busy with the ranch work now to do it. Maybe next year.

July 12: Oh drat. The lunch burned again today. Loper injured his gums chewing the meat loaf. He also wondered if I had spilled the pepper shaker in the potatoes. I smiled. He coughed and drank some water.

© G.L. Holmes

Later that day: The boys started working on the utility room right after lunch. Loper had planned to do some windmill work but decided it could wait.

July 15: We have a new utility room. I didn't realize that cowboys could be so handy with a hammer and nails. All these years Loper has told me that hammering irritates his roping elbow. I'm glad to know that we have such talent on the ranch.

The boys are taking their boots off in the utility room now. The lunch did not burn today. I served them a nice juicy apple pie for dessert, and while they wolfed it down, I mentioned that I need a pickup-load of manure on the fall garden. Moments after I said this, the boys grabbed their hats and went to work on the windmill.

Poor Slim is a slow eater and was not able to finish his pie.

August 24: My darling husband came in last night with injuries received in the line of duty. Here is the story he told me.

Along toward evening, he was riding the home pasture, checking the steers. He found a sick one in the willows down along the creek. He tried to drive the steer out of the brush and to the corral, but the steer did not want to go.

Instead, he waded out into the middle of the creek and stood there. My husband is not a patient man. God bless him, he has a heart of purest gold, but every once in a while he will throw a temper tantrum. When we were first married, he kicked a horse and broke his toe. I thought this might have reformed him. Apparently not.

He rode into the creek and tried to drive the steer out on the bank. The steer sulled. This kind of behavior angers my husband. He is trying to keep the animals alive, and sometimes he feels they are trying to commit suicide.

He decided he would drag the steer out of the water. He roped him and turned Happy to pull. Alas, in his anger he forgot to tighten the cinch. The saddle ended up on Happy's side. My true love landed in the creek, with an undallied rope in his hand, and his faithful horse ran back to the barn.

What followed next is an amazing tale. The steer decided to run. My husband held on to the rope and was dragged through the mud and water. When he managed to get his hands on the beast, they were standing in water three feet deep.

The steer was ready to fight by this time, and, God love him, so was my husband. The steer pinned him against a mud bank and butted him in the chest, while Loper pummeled him on the nose with both fists. The fight ended in a draw, with both too exhausted to move.

Loper dragged himself back home, stripped off his clothes on the porch, and came into the house wearing boxer shorts and a cowboy hat. His hands were swollen and he had bruises on his chest.

But mainly, I think, his pride was damaged. He wanted sympathy and became quite angry when I laughed. I would have sooner cut out my tongue than wound his pride further, but I doubt that any human on earth could have listened to that incredible story without laughing.

No one, that is, but my husband. He did not see the humor at all.

I tried to be sympathetic. I put ice packs on his hands and rubbed Ben-Gay on his chest. I stroked his brow and assured him that any grown man could have gotten into a fist fight with a steer.

He fell asleep on the living room floor. In sleep, his face was serene. I am amazed at the healing power of a woman's touch. I am equally amazed at the childish vanity and animal stubbornness of a Texas cowboy.

I suspect that a cowboy grows up just in time to scold his grandchildren for doing exactly what he did only a few years before.

August 26: At lunch, I casually mentioned that it is past time to plant the fall garden. The silence that followed this statement was remarkable.

August 27: Subtlety has not worked on the manure issue. I was forced to be blunt. I pointed out to my husband that I have bought twenty dollars' worth of seed, and that it is getting late in the season.

To my astonishment, he yielded the point. Yes, he said, we sure need to get the garden in. I could hardly believe my ears. But I soon understood.

My husband's hands were still sore from his boxing match with the steer, so he volunteered Slim for the manure detail. Slim almost bit his fork in two when he heard this. There was an exchange of glances between them. When Slim stomped outside, I heard him mutter, "I thought I hired onto this outfit to be a cowboy, not to shovel . . . "

The door slammed and I did not hear the rest.

Later that day: Slim sulked and growled all afternoon. Every time he threw a scoop of manure into the pickup, he cursed it. But he spread it on the garden very nicely. At five o'clock I called him up for lemonade and cookies fresh out of the oven. Before long, he was laughing.

As I recall, it was Archimedes who said, "Give me a place to rest my lever and I will move the earth." I believe a cowboy could do the same with a scoop shovel or a hammer, if you could just give him enough cookies and pie.

Confessions of a Cowdog:
Part Two

It's me again, Hank the cowdog. I keep getting into trouble around here. I don't know what's wrong. I try to run this ranch the way it ought to be run, but I don't get much cooperation.

Take the boss as an example. He ain't what you'd call fond of dogs. First thing in the morning he'll come walking down to the corral. Most of the time I'm already down there, checking things out. I'm in charge of ranch security, don't you see, and that's such an important job, I like to get out early and make my morning rounds.

So into the corral walks the boss with a scowl on his face. I come up to him, wagging my tail and grinning and trying to be about half-friendly. What does he do? He gives me this greeting: "Go on, dog, git outa here."

Every day it's the same. I don't have to do anything wrong. He just looks at me and those words come to his lips. I don't understand it.

Well, all right, maybe I do, just a little bit. I've made a few mistakes, but they were honest mistakes, nothing he should hold a grudge about.

I guess my troubles with the boss go back to that day last summer. I got myself locked in the saddle shed. Drover, my running buddy, had told me that there was a mouse in there, and as head of ranch security, I figured it was my duty to go in and check it out. Pete the cat is supposed to be in charge of mice, but you can't depend on a danged cat for anything.

So I was in there sniffing in a corner, and the next thing I knew, the cowboys turned out the light and locked the door. That was a bad deal, me locked up and night coming on and no one out there to guard the ranch.

I knew Drover couldn't handle it by himself. He's pretty tough as long as I'm out front doing the fighting and the dirty work, but when I'm not around, he goes up and hides in the machine shed. He won't even bark at the mailman in broad daylight unless I'm there.

Well, I got in a big sweat worrying about it. What if robbers came in the night? What if the steers came up around the house and started rubbing on Sally May's evergreen trees? Suppose the coons pulled a sneak attack, or the coyotes came up around the house and woke up High Loper? When Loper misses his sleep, he ain't fit to live with.

I had to get out of there, that was all there was to it. The ranch was in danger. I reviewed the situation and decided there was only one way out: I would have to chew a hole in the door.

I went right to work. I chewed and I chewed and I spit out pieces of wood and I got a splinter in my gum and it took me an hour to get it out. And then I chewed some more.

About daylight, I had a fair-sized hole built in the door, but it wasn't quite big enough. Then I heard a pickup outside. Someone got out and coughed. I said to myself, "Ah ha, they've missed me and they've come to let me out."

The door opened and there was the boss. He looked down at my work and looked at me. His face went red and he roared, "Dangit, you're eatin' the door off the saddle shed, get outa here!"

That's the thanks I got for trying to do my job. Did he think I chewed up the door just because I like the taste of wood?

He took off his hat and started swinging it at me. "Go on, git outa here!" I would have been glad to get out. I had spent all night trying to get out. But since he was standing in the door and swatting at me with his hat, I couldn't get out.

That just made him madder. I dashed around the saddle shed, knocked a saddle off the rack and spilled a can of neat's foot oil. At last, I ran between his legs and escaped. He throwed a hoof pick at me but missed.

Well, that got his nose out of joint, and he stayed mad for the rest of the morning. We might have patched things up, but we got into another wreck that afternoon.

The boss and High Loper were sorting cows in the front lot after dinner. I was lying outside the corral, taking a little snooze in the sun and catching up on all the sleep I'd missed the night before.

Pete, the barn cat, came up and started playing

with my tail. I raised my head and told him to buzz off. He kept it up. He was swatting my tail with his paws. It didn't hurt and I tried to ignore it. But then he sank his claws in and struck a nerve.

I can get along with anybody's cat as long as he knows his place. His place, as far as I'm concerned, is either out of my sight or up a tree. My second-most important job on this outfit, after ranch security, is keeping the cats humble and in their place. I don't take no trash off a cat.

I growled and gave Pete fair warning. "Best leave my tail alone, son. Run along and play. I've got important things to do."

He looked at me and kind of cocked his head to the side. Then, out of sheer spite, he slapped my tail again.

Drover had been watching from under the pick-up, and he came galloping up. His hair was bristled up on the back of his neck and he was showing his fangs. "Get lost, squirt, or we'll . . . "

Bam! Before Drover could finish his sentence, Pete slapped him across the chops. He yelped and moved out of range.

"You're just lucky I didn't pull off one of your legs and beat you to death with it," said Drover. Pete yawned. "Look at him, Hank, see what he did? He's got no respect for a cowdog."

Ordinarily I would have just whipped the cat and got it over with, but I needed some sleep. I laid my head back down and fell right to sleep. I was twitching and rolling my eyes and having a wonderful dream, when I felt a sharp pain in my tail.

Drover was right there, whispering in my ear. "It was the cat again, Hank, I seen him. He was playing with your tail, after you told him not to."

"Will you shut up? I know what he did." I stood up and went nose-to-nose with Pete. "Cat, you're fixing to get yourself into a storm."

"Git, 'im, Hank, git 'im!"

"I done told you to lay off the tail and buzz off. Now, are you gonna buzz or do I need to give you your daily whipping?"

"You tell him, Hankie, preach that hot gospel!"

I looked back at Drover, who was jumping up and down in excitement. "Will you just shut your little trap and let me handle this?" Back to the cat. "What's it gonna be, son? Peace and quiet or blood and guts?"

Pete throwed a hump into his back and hissed, right in my face, which is one of about twenty-three things I don't allow a cat to get by with. Then he popped me on the nose, and the fight was on.

I lit right in the middle of him and had him buried, but he squirmed out and somehow popped me on the nose again. It made my eyes water, it stung so bad.

Drover was jumping around in circles. "Git 'im, Hankie, tear him up!"

Couldn't quite get a handle on the squirmy little son of a gun. I chased him around the pickup once, then he ducked under the fence and ran into the front lot—where the cowboys were sorting cattle. I was in hot pursuit.

Well, one thing led to another. I ran right in front of this snorty old cow, don't you see, and the next thing I knew, she was blowing hot air on the back of my neck and shaking her horns at me. It sort of took my mind off the cat.

I ran for the nearest cover, which happened to be the boss, and you might say that he got plastered. The old cow took aim for me and got the boss instead. Bedded him down slick as a whistle.

Then I did my duty as a loyal cowdog. I rushed to his side and licked him in the face. He turned red and screeched, "Dammittohell, git outa here!"

I can take a hint. I know when I'm not welcome. I got the heck out of there.

Who do you reckon got the blame for this? Pete, who started the whole thing? The cow, who did the actual damage? No, no. Good old easy-going, fun-loving, hard-working Hank.

And ever since that time, when me and the boss run into each other, he don't say howdy or good morning. It's "Go on, dog, git outa here."

It's hard, being a cowdog. You've got to take trash off the cats and abuse from the cattle, and you get no thanks, no respect from the boss. I guess that's why they keep me around this ranch, so that any time somebody fouls up, they can call in old Hank and pin the blame on him. It's a cruel old world.

The Devil in Texas

After lunch, me and High Loper usually curl up on the floor of the ranch house and take a short nap. It kind of settles our grub and gives us a fresh attitude about the afternoon's work.

The other day we ate several bowls of hot spiced chili, and while we were eating, one of my favorite songs came on the radio. It was Charlie Daniels' "Devil Down in Georgia."

I don't know whether it was the chili or the song that did it, but during naptime I had an outrageous dream.

Me and Loper were ahorseback, riding through one of the pastures north of headquarters. It was a cold winter day. The prairie country was brown and bare, and the old cottonwoods reached like skeleton hands toward a brooding gray sky.

As usual, we were playing with our ropes as we

75

rode along. Loper was mounted on a big sorrel named Happy, and I came along behind on my little Calipso mare. Loper was pitching his rope on soapweeds, and I was right behind him heeling his horse.

Old Hap was the kind of horse that was always looking for boogers. He'd shy from a cow chip, walk around a little sand rat hole, or fly over a trickle of water. So we weren't particularly surprised when all at once he dropped his head, stretched out his neck, perked his ears, snorted, and started running sideways. But when Calipso did the same thing, it made us a little curious.

We got our broncs under control and did some heavy spurring to get them back to the rock ledge where the runaway had started. We thought we might find a porcupine or maybe a dead calf.

What we saw was a little guy sitting on a donkey. He had his right leg thrown over the horn of his saddle, and he was rolling a Prince Albert cigarette. His face was skinny and sharp pointed, his skin as red as a hot branding iron.

He didn't wear a hat, and it was easy to see why. He had two horns coming out the sides of his bald head. He was ugly—ugly as the very devil.

Me and Loper traded glances, as if to say, "What is this?" The man lapped his cigarette and lit up. When he snapped his fingers, a flame appeared out of his thumb.

"Afternoon, boys," he said in a high, squeaky voice.

We nodded. Old Happy was pointing this guy like a bird dog. He'd spent his whole life looking for boogers, and by George he'd finally found one.

"My name's John Devil," said the man. "I come

from Hell and I can out-ride, out-rope, out-cuss, and out-spit any cowboy I ever met."

Loper kind of grinned. "Well, if that's true, Mr. Devil, then you've spent too much time in Hell and Kansas. This here's the Texas Panhandle, and me and my partner have never been out-rode or out-roped. Nobody ever tried us on the spittin' and cussin'."

Old Devil laughed to himself and looked at Loper's horse. "Do you milk that thing or use him strictly for plow work?" Then he looked at my mare. "Kind of a cute little thing. If she ever grows into them long skinny legs, she's liable to stand twenty-seven hands at the withers."

Me and Loper don't mind personal insults, but bad-mouthing the horseflesh is hard to forgive, especially when it comes from a man on a donkey.

"We manage to get the work done," I said.

"I'm surprised."

Loper shifted his quid to the other cheek. "You're fixing to be more than that."

"Tell you what let's do, boys. Let's have us a little roping contest, Hell against Texas."

"Hell against Texas is a normal day around here," I said. "What else you got in mind?"

"You see that steer?" Devil pointed his finger and a *corriente* steer suddenly appeared on the flat below. "One loop apiece, head, half-head, or horns."

"What's the stakes?"

Devil arched his brows. "Your souls, fellers, your souls. If you both miss and I catch, you got to work for me. We just can't find good help in Hell any more."

"What if we win?"

He untied his catch rope and held it up. "You get

this rope. It's made of threads of pure gold, and it's worth a fortune."

It isn't every day that a cowboy gets a chance to make a fortune. We told old Devil to kiss his rope good-bye, and we went charging down the hill toward the steer, just the way we do when we're doctoring sick cattle. First man there gets first throw, and the second man stands by for a second throw or heels.

Calipso and I got there first. When the old steer saw us coming, he stuck out his tail and made a dash for the creek. He ran straight and fast, just the kind of shot I like. I knew I couldn't miss. Calipso put me right on top of him. I swung my loop and floated out a nice flat, open noose.

But at the last second, as if by magic, a gust of wind came up. My loop hit the left horn and fell into the dirt. "Get him, Loper!" I yelled over my shoulder.

Loper and Happy were hot on his tail. Loper swung and threw a pretty noose, but the same thing happened to him. A strong gust of wind came up and the loop died in the air.

We heard a squeal of laughter behind us, and here came John Devil and his donkey. "Out of the way, Texas! Here's how we do it in Hell!"

That warn't no ordinary donkey. He was as fast as a racehorse. He caught up with that Mexican steer in a hurry, and when he did, John Devil did a strange thing. He turned clear around in the saddle so that he was riding backward. When the donkey flew past the steer, Mr. Devil pitched the golden rope around his horns, put the end of the rope between his teeth, and jerked the steer plumb out of his tracks.

It wasn't the sort of thing a normal man could get by with.

"You know," I said to Loper, "there's something funny going on around here."

"Yalp. A guy might think that old Devil was cheatin'."

"A guy sure might."

"You want to work in Hell?"

"Nope."

"What do you think?"

"Let's do it."

John Devil came riding up to us, coiling up his golden rope and chuckling to himself. "Tough luck, boys. Pack your bags, we're going to . . ."

"Hell if we are," said Loper. We had our loops built. "We're fixing to do a little pasture work."

John Devil glanced at me and then at Loper. He'd never seen such a wicked pair of faces, not in Hell or Kansas or anywhere else he'd been. "Now boys . . . " He stuck the spurs in that donkey and hauled for the caprock.

I was dallied when the slack went out of my rope. The donkey kept going, but John Devil came to a sudden stop, seeing as how I had a nice little loop fitted around his horns.

He squalled and bellered and kicked and pitched, but Loper scooted a big old circle of nylon around his middle and picked up both hocks. We stretched him out, throwed half-hitches over our dallies, and met in the middle, each of us packing a medicine bag.

"What do you reckon?" said Loper. "Pinkeye?" I said yep, so we squirted both eyes with blue drops and glued on a couple of eye patches.

"Loper, I think he's bloated too." We got the rubber hose and ran it down his guzzle.

"And he's kinder droopy in his ears." So we gave him fifteen cc's of Combiotic and a couple of big sulfa pills for good measure.

Just then I felt somebody shaking my shoulder. I opened my eyes and saw High Loper and his mustache. "Wake up. What's the matter with you? You're over here gruntin' like a bunch of hogs."

I sat up and eased out a burp of garlic and chili powder. Or maybe it was gun powder. "Brother, I had a bad dream."

"About what?"

"Well, we was out roping and . . . "

"Hold it right there. I know you're lying."

"Huh?"

Loper smashed my cowboy hat down on my head. "Any dream with roping in it ain't bad. Let's go to work."

The World's First Cowboy

In the beginning, God created the heavens and the earth. And He said, "Let the waters under the heavens be gathered together into one place, and let the dry land appear."

The dry land appeared, and it was very dry. He called it Texas.

And God said, "Let the earth bring forth living creatures: cattle and creeping things and beasts of the earth." And it was so.

Then God said, "Let us make man in our own image and give him dominion over the earth." So God created man and put him in Texas.

And God said, "Let us call this man Adam and give him a horse." And it was so. God placed him astride the horse and saw that it was good.

Then God planted a garden in Eden, in East Texas, and there He put the man he had formed. He made to grow every tree that is pleasant to the sight and good for food, and He populated the garden with all the beasts of the earth.

Among the beasts was the cow. And God said to Adam, "You may subdue every beast of the field and fowl of the air, but do not bother the cow, for it is special."

Then God said, "It is not good that the man should be alone. I will make him a helper." And God caused a sleep to fall upon the man and took one of his ribs and made it into a woman. God showed her to the man and asked if he was pleased.

And the man replied, "Yee-ha, woopee, mercy, mercy, mercy!" And God knew that it was good.

Now, the serpent was more subtle than any other wild creature that the Lord had made, and one day he appeared to the woman.

"Why do you not subdue the cow? She can yield milk and cream that can be made into cheese and butter. And she will bring forth calves for meat."

And Eve replied, "We are forbidden to bother the cow. God has told us not to, and He would be angry if we did."

And the serpent said, "Surely you misunderstood. God would not make a cow and put it in the garden if He did not want you to use it."

Eve was troubled by this and spoke to Adam about it. "No, it is forbidden," he said, "but let me talk to the snake." He found the snake and they talked.

And the snake replied, "If God had really wanted you to leave the cow alone, he wouldn't have given you that horse."

"The horse? What does the horse have to do with it?"

"Well," said the snake, "if you train the horse, you can make the cow go anywhere you want her to go."

"I didn't know that," said Adam.

So he took a vine and put it into the horse's mouth and tied forked sticks on his heels and climbed on the horse's back. He stuck the sticks into the animal's sides and said, "Gitty up." And, lo, the horse erupted and threw Adam into the tree of knowledge.

Adam returned to the serpent and said, "This will not work. The horse is much bigger than I and he does not wish to cooperate."

The serpent said, "It is written that when a man is thrown from a horse, he must climb back on before he is frozen by fear."

"I am already frozen by fear," said Adam, "but I shall try again."

And he climbed upon the horse and the horse did buck and Adam did stay on his back. And the woman cheered for him and said that she was proud.

So Adam and the horse went forth into the garden. He drove the cow around and around, just as the serpent had predicted. But when he got down from the horse and tried to catch her, she ran away.

He returned to the snake. "It does me no good to ride the horse to drive the cow, for she will not let me milk her."

And the serpent spake, saying, "God has made the grass, and the grass shall provide you with a tool. Cut it, weave it together, and make a rope."

Adam did as he was told, and when he had made a rope, he returned to the serpent. And he said, "Here is the rope. What does it do?"

And the serpent showed him how to build a

loop, how to throw a hoolihan and a Blocker, how to catch forelegs and heels.

But Adam said, "Surely this is wrong. God has told us not to subdue the cow."

And the serpent said, "If God had not wanted you to rope, he would not have made grass."

So Adam went forth and roped the cow, and while he held her, Eve drew milk from her bag. And when she had finished, Adam let the cow go and roped her again, this time just for fun. And, lo, he spent the entire day, roping the cow.

That evening, Adam and Eve heard God walking through the garden, and they hid themselves from His presence, for they knew they had done wrong and were afraid.

"Where are you?" God called. They did not answer, but He saw the cow, with an empty bag and rope burns around her horns. And He was angry and He called them in a voice of thunder. "What have you done?"

Adam came out, hiding the rope behind his back. "Well, you see, my wife . . . "

Then Eve appeared and said, "No, no. You see, my husband . . . "

And then they both spake in unison, "It was the snake that made us do it."

God rebuked the serpent, gave him poisoned fangs and a rattle on his tail, and ordered him to crawl on his belly for ever and ever.

And to Eve He said, "Because you have not listened to me, I shall make your husband a cowboy. He will work long hours in the heat of summer and the cold of winter, and he shall receive low wages."

And to Adam, He said, "Because you have not

listened to me, because you have chosen to chase cattle, I shall smite the cow-brute in the brain and make it stupid. You shall spend your days working with stupid animals.

"And I am giving you a more serious curse. Here is a plow. With it you will till the ground and plant crops. At the very time when you want to go rope cattle, you will have to plow and plant."

Adam cried and begged God not to give him the plow, but God heard him not. Then He said, "You are naked. Make yourselves some clothes, for you must leave the garden."

"Where will we go?"

"I shall drive you to the ends of the earth, beyond the wilderness and the desert, to the place where the wind moans across an empty land."

"Not the Panhandle!"

"Yes, the Panhandle. Go!"

So Eve sewed fig leaves together and made a dress for herself. And for Adam, she made a pair of shotgun chaps. And with the Lord pointing the way with a fiery sword, they climbed upon the horse and drove the cow away from the garden. When they reached the ends of the earth, they knew they had arrived in the Panhandle.

There they stopped and made a home. The cow brought forth calves, and lo, they were stupid. Adam could not support his wife and children with the cattle and had to use the plow. Following the plow day after day, he dreamed of roping calves, and he felt the sting of God's curse.

(*Author's note:* This ain't exactly the same story that appears in the Bible, but it helps to explain a lot about cowboys and rattlesnakes.)

A Windy Tale

It was one of them typical beautiful spring days in the Texas Panhandle, the kind we get around the middle of March.

The grass was trying to green up. The cottonwoods and elms down along Bitter Creek were putting out buds. And I guess the birds were chirping, if a guy could have heard them. But a guy couldn't hear them because of the wind.

The wind was on a ripping, roaring, hell-bending, dust-blowing snort. The radio in the pickup said it was moving along at forty to fifty miles an hour, with gusts up to sixty-five. Me and High Loper were trying to feed cattle in that wind, and it was pretty discouraging work.

We fed some 20% cake to the steers up in the north pastures. Steers are hard to feed under the best of circumstances, because they're so dumb. Sometimes they won't come up to feed. When you blow the pickup horn, they'll stand out there and stare at you, as if they can't quite understand why two grown men would be bouncing across the pasture and blowing a horn.

Other times, they'll come up and chase the pickup, as any normal starving cow brute would do. But when you pour the feed out on the ground, they run right over it and never find it. Then they all bunch up and mill around and bawl because they're hungry.

That's what you call *dumb* dumb, and in steers it's typical behavior.

But feeding in that high wind was even worse. The steers were bunched up down in the holes and canyons. Half of them couldn't hear the horn. The other half heard it but didn't want to crawl out of their holes and fight the wind. We stared at them and they stared at us. We cussed at them for being too dumb to come for grub, and who knows? Maybe they were laughing at us for getting out in a sixty mile an hour wind.

Course me and Loper had an excuse. We were hired hands on a ranch, and we drew wages for doing foolish things.

We didn't have much luck with the steers. We called a few out of the canyons and throwed them some grub. Loper put the pickup in grandma-low and drove, while I sat on the tailgate and strung out the feed. When I got back into the pickup, my eyes were full of 20% cake crumbs, and I had grit on my teeth. I had my straw hat tied down with a piece of string, otherwise it would have been up around Seward County, Kansas, heading toward Nebraska.

"What a lousy day," I grumbled. I spit the dirt

out of my mouth and looked up at the reddish haze in the sky. "There's lots of real estate changing hands today."

Loper grunted. "I'm sick of wind and dirt and hay and feeding cattle. A cowboy shouldn't have to put up with this kind of nonsense."

Naturally I agreed. Me and Loper considered ourselves cowboys, a cut or two above the average mortal. We loved to ride and rope, listen to our spurs jingle and wear gaudy clothes. But we hadn't been ahorseback in two weeks, hadn't thrown a rope in three. We'd been feeding the danged cattle.

We drove down out of the north pastures and headed for the hay stack. We'd fed the steers, more or less, and now we had to load up fifty bales of alfalfa for the cows. Loper backed up to the stack and we opened our doors to get out. The wind caught Loper's door. He hung on and it jerked him clean out of his seat. I managed to get out and shut mine before it got un-hinged.

I went around to the front of the pickup and joined him. He was looking up at the top of the stack, and I knew what he was thinking: somebody had to crawl up there and throw off bales, and that somebody would run the risk of getting himself blowed into the middle pasture.

"I guess you want to throw and I'll stack," I yelled over the wind, and got a mouthful of alfalfa leaves.

Loper grinned, as if to say that I had guessed wrong. He dug a quarter out of his jeans. "Heads or tails?"

I thought it over. I'd never had any luck with heads, so I called tails. He flipped the coin with his thumb. The wind caught it and we had to chase it down. It came up heads, which is fairly typical of the way my life has gone these past thirty-seven years.

I pulled my hat down to my ears and started crawling up the stack. The higher I got, the harder the wind blew. When I reached the top layer, I could hardly stand up. I grabbed a bale by the wires and staggered toward the edge of the stack. I hefted it up on my knees and threw it out just as hard as I could.

Seems to me there's a law of physics which says that when you throw a bale of hay south, you throw yourself north at the same time. I went stumbling backward and a big gust of wind caught me. I hooked the heel of my left boot on a hay wire, and it was *adios* and *buenas noches* for me.

I went over the side, fifteen feet straight down, and landed in the middle of the hay baler. Must have knocked me out.

I had a crazy dream. I saw me and Loper roping steers on a white sandy beach, with palm trees on one side and the turquoise ocean on the other. Four or five beautiful girls watched us from the palm trees, and every time we headed and double-hocked a steer, they came running out to us, put flowers around our necks and gave us kisses and forced us to drink a concoction made of coconut milk and liquor. We drank it through a straw, right out of the coconut.

On this beach, there was no wind and not a sign of a haystack.

It was one of my better moments on the ranch. I didn't want to wake up.

But the laughter of the girls faded away and changed into Loper's hacksaw voice. "Come on, Slim, wake up boy. We got cattle to feed."

I opened my eyes a crack. I was laying across the baler. The sky was dirty brown. The wind was howling. Loper was fanning me with his hat. Seemed a little odd that he'd want to fan me with his hat, when the wind was about to blow my ears off.

I sat up and shook my head. "What happened?"

"Hay baler jumped up on the stack and grabbed you. You hurt?"

I moved around a little bit. Everything hurt. "Not enough to count. Loper, let's me and you start watching the help wanted ads and find us a steer operation on a tropical island where we can lay around under the palm trees and rope cattle on the beach. I've just about decided that I could be happy with a deal like that."

He stared at me. I told him about my dream. Neither one of us noticed that the bossman had pulled up in his pickup, until he gunned his motor and we heard the fan belt squeal.

"Afternoon, gentlemen. I hope I'm not interrupting anything."

He was smiling, but a guy got the feeling that it was forced.

"Oh no, that's all right," said Loper.

"Just got back from town," said the boss. "Looked at some new hay equipment, an outfit that makes a self-propelled bale."

"Never heard of it."

"Well, you put the bales in the stack, and come winter, they grow legs and walk out to the pasture. I figgered that might be the only way we'd get these cattle fed."

He rolled up his window and drove off. Loper looked at me.

"What did he mean by that?"

"Beats me. Was it a hint of some kind?"

"I couldn't tell. He's too subtle for me." He looked up to the top of the stack. "Well, I'll try it this time."

"Watch out for that baler. It'll sure grab you." He started climbing, then stopped. "You reckon a guy could find a cowboy job in Acapulco?"

"I bet he could, Loper. We'll start watching the ads."